MW01293743

Specific Skill Series

Working Within Words

Richard A. Boning

Fifth Edition

SRA/McGraw-Hill
Columbus, Ohio

Cover, Back Cover, Ron Sanford / The Stock Market

SRA/McGraw-Hill

*A Division of The **McGraw·Hill** Companies*

Printed in the United States of America.

Send all inquiries to:
    SRA/McGraw-Hill
    8787 Orion Place
    Columbus, OH 43240-4027

ISBN 0-02-687921-2

    5 6 7 IPC 02 01 00

To the Teacher

PURPOSE:

WORKING WITHIN WORDS helps pupils put sounds and other word elements to work to determine word meaning. Many units in WORKING WITHIN WORDS develop understandings about sound-symbol (phonic) associations. Other units treat letter combinations, syllabication, roots and affixes, accent patterns, compound words, longer words, and spelling changes caused by adding endings.

FOR WHOM:

The skill of WORKING WITHIN WORDS is developed through a series of books spanning ten levels (Picture, Preparatory, A, B, C, D, E, F, G, H). The Picture Level is for pupils who have not acquired a basic sight vocabulary. The Preparatory Level is for pupils who have a basic sight vocabulary but are not yet ready for the first-grade-level book. Books A through H are appropriate for pupils who can read on levels one through eight, respectively. **The use of the *Specific Skill Series Placement Test* is recommended to determine the appropriate level.**

THE NEW EDITION:

The fifth edition of the *Specific Skill Series* maintains the quality and focus that has distinguished this program for more than 25 years. A key element central to the program's success has been the unique nature of the reading selections. Nonfiction pieces about current topics have been designed to stimulate the interest of students, motivating them to use the comprehension strategies they have learned to further their reading. To keep this important aspect of the program intact, a percentage of the reading selections have been replaced in order to ensure the continued relevance of the subject material.

In addition, a significant percentage of the artwork in the program has been replaced to give the books a contemporary look. The cover photographs are designed to appeal to readers of all ages.

SESSIONS:

Short practice sessions are the most effective. It is desirable to have a practice session every day or every other day, using a few units each session.

SCORING:

Pupils should record their answers on the reproducible worksheets. The worksheets make scoring easier and provide uniform records of the pupils' work. Using worksheets also avoids consuming the exercise books.

It is important for pupils to know how well they are doing. For this reason, units should be scored as soon as they have been completed. Then a discussion can be held in which pupils justify their choices. (The Integrated Language Activities, many of which are open-ended, do not lend themselves to an objective score; thus there are no answer keys for these pages.)

GENERAL INFORMATION ON *WORKING WITHIN WORDS*:

The units are of two types: concept builders and functional exercises. The concept units focus the reader's attention on common patterns and parts of words. Each generalization is built step-by-step on the structure of previously formed concepts. The functional exercises either follow the concept units or are contained within them. They provide the reader with many immediate and repeated experiences with words involving particular patterns or principles. Sentence settings are typical for the pupils' level; often the choices offered are new words.

As WORKING WITHIN WORDS progresses through different word elements there is constant reinforcement. The more elementary booklets focus on phonic elements such as consonant sounds, consonant substitutions, blends, phonograms, and vowel sounds. As the level of difficulty increases, the emphasis shifts to syllabication, prefixes, suffixes, and roots.

A unit-by-unit list of concepts developed in this book is found on page 64.

INSTRUCTIONS:

Minimal direction is required. Pupils' attention must be drawn to the answer choices. In the concept units only two or three answer choices are offered. In the units that provide application of understandings, four to nine answer choices are offered, providing more experiences with words of a particular pattern. In units which offer an *F* choice, the *F* stands for NONE. This means that none of the choices makes sense in that particular setting.

RELATED MATERIALS:

Specific Skill Series Placement Tests, which enable the teacher to place pupils at their appropriate levels in each skill, are available for the Elementary (Pre-1–6) and Midway (4–8) grade levels.

As you learn to read, you learn the sounds that letters stand for in words. First, you look at the letters in a word. Next, you put together the sounds for the letters. Then you can tell what the word is.

You can think of a word as a kind of secret message written in code. And you are a spy trying to find the meaning of that secret message. You are trying to **decode** the word. The sounds the letters stand for are the key to unlocking the code.

Knowing the sounds of a word is only a beginning. Just as a secret message may have many parts, a word may have more than one part, too. In order to read and understand a word, you need to understand the parts of the word. For example, when you add the ending *s* to a naming word, it changes the word to mean "more than one." It is the difference between *one cat* and *three cats*.

In this book, you will work with words in different ways. For some pages, you will tell which picture name goes in the blank in a sentence. For other pages, you will choose the correct word to complete a sentence. Sometimes the clue to correct answers is the first or last letter in a word. Sometimes the clue is a word ending.

When you know the sounds that letters stand for, you will have one key to the code. When you know how word parts change the meaning of a word, you will have another key. You will be able to unlock the meaning of most written words.

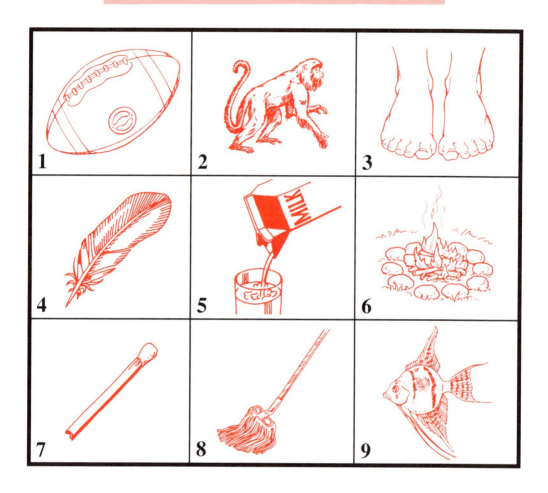

1. The **m**_____ likes to run and jump.

2. We cleaned the floor with a **m**_____.

3. The **f**_____ is in the water.

4. The **f**_____ is very hot.

5. Jenny and Ed like to play **f**_____.

6. I like to drink **m**_____ with cake.

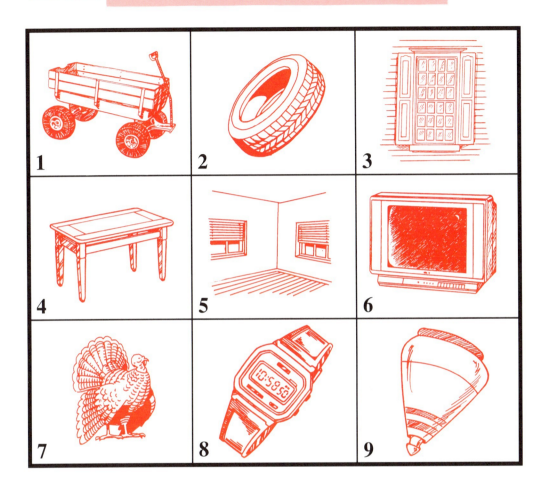

1. Mother got a **t**_____ for the car.

2. My **w**_____ tells me the time.

3. Place the food on the **t**_____.

4. We saw the big **t**_____ at the farm.

5. Sam rides in the little **w**_____.

6. I like to look out the **w**_____.

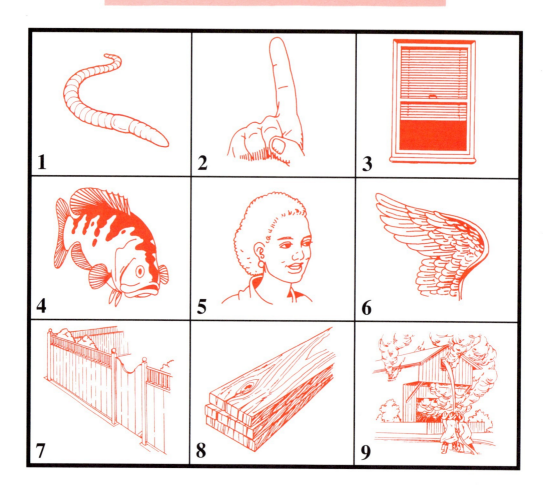

1. We saw a big house on **f**_____ .

2. Who is that **w**_____ ?

3. Did you cut your **f**_____ ?

4. The house is made of **w**_____ .

5. That bird hurt its **w**_____ .

6. There is a **f**_____ around my yard.

1. Juan likes to play in the **t**_____.

2. I saw the **m**_____ at night.

3. My father will wear his new **t**_____.

4. A **m**_____ came to see the teacher.

5. The red **t**_____ was good to eat.

6. Sue and I have a pet **m**_____.

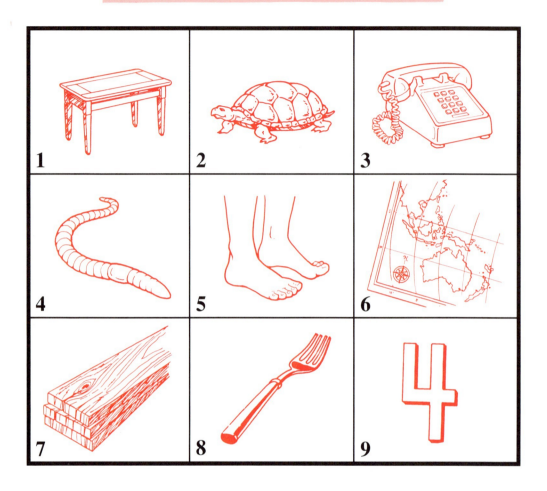

1. We can eat it with a **f**_____ .

2. The hen was eating a **w**_____ .

3. I did not find it on the **m**_____ .

4. A **t**_____ can not walk very fast.

5. Did you hear the **t**_____ ring?

6. There were **f**_____ people in the car.

1. I helped take care of the **b**_____.

2. The **c**_____ tells us the day.

3. She likes to ride on her **b**_____.

4. Betty will make a **c**_____ for me.

5. Jack will throw the **b**_____ to Pam.

6. She is wearing her new **c**_____.

1. A s_____ likes to ride on a boat.

2. You can't see the s_____ in the sky.

3. My grandfather always wears a h_____.

4. They walked into the h_____.

5. Jack will wear his new s_____.

6. Did you cut your h_____?

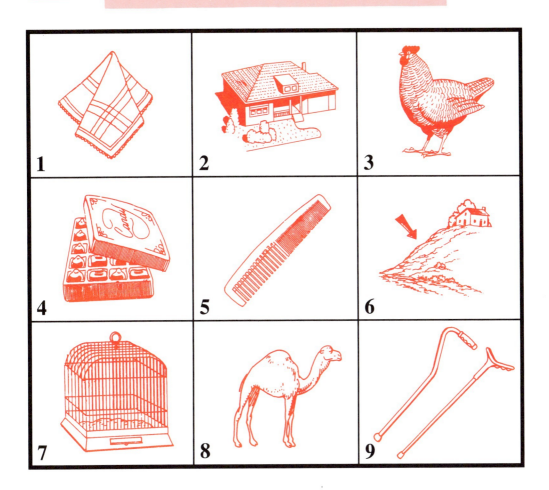

1. Ron got his mother a box of **c**_____ .

2. We will walk up the **h**_____ .

3. I always carry a **h**_____ in my pocket.

4. What do you feed the **h**_____?

5. Who wants to ride on a **c**_____?

6. The bird flew out of the **c**_____ .

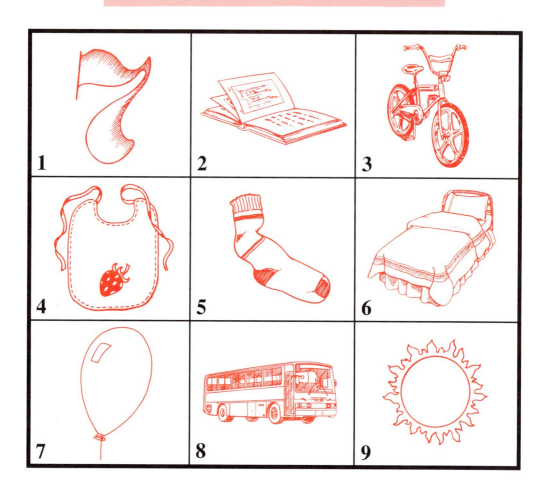

1. Jim blew up a big red **b**_____ .

2. I lost one **s**_____ and one shoe.

3. Mother put a **b**_____ on the baby.

4. At night I jump into **b**_____ .

5. There are **s**_____ days in a week.

6. I went for a ride on my **b**_____ .

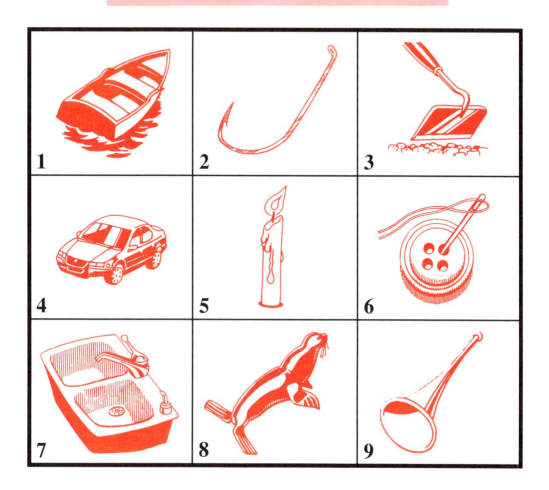

1. See the new **c**_____ on the street.

2. They saw a **s**_____ in the water.

3. Put the worm on the **h**_____.

4. Wash your hands in the **s**_____.

5. Lee put a **b**_____ on her coat.

6. The **b**_____ is in the water.

1. Mother went up on a **l**_____ .

2. Is a **l**_____ a good pet?

3. The **l**_____ helps us see at night.

4. There is a new **r**_____ on the floor.

5. Sue can go fast on her **r**_____ .

6. I saw the little **r**_____ run away.

1. On the farm we saw a **p**_____.

2. Mother put the car into the **g**_____.

3. "I like to chew **g**_____," said Jan.

4. Pat will make a **p**_____ for us.

5. She is a pretty **g**_____.

6. Mary likes to play the **p**_____.

A. Exercising Your Skill

Name each picture below. Listen to the beginning sound.

Write the letter that stands for the beginning sound.

List three other words that begin with the same sound as each of the pictures.

B. Expanding Your Skill

Play "eraser toss." Write each of these letters on a sheet of paper: m b s p h c

Tape the sheets together. Put them on the floor.

Make two teams. Take turns tossing an eraser onto the paper. Say a word that begins with the letter the eraser lands on.

Score 1 point for each word and 2 points if the word names something you can wear. The team with more points at the end wins.

C. Exploring Language

Add the missing letters to complete these riddles.

1. I sit on your head.
   I am your __at.

2. I hug your hands and keep them warm.
   I am your __ittens.

3. You walk on me, but it does not hurt me.
   I am your __ocks.

4. I have two legs, just like you.
   I have pockets too.
   I am your __ants.

D. Expressing Yourself

Draw two pictures of children playing outside.
Make one show summertime. Make one show winter.
Label what the children are wearing.

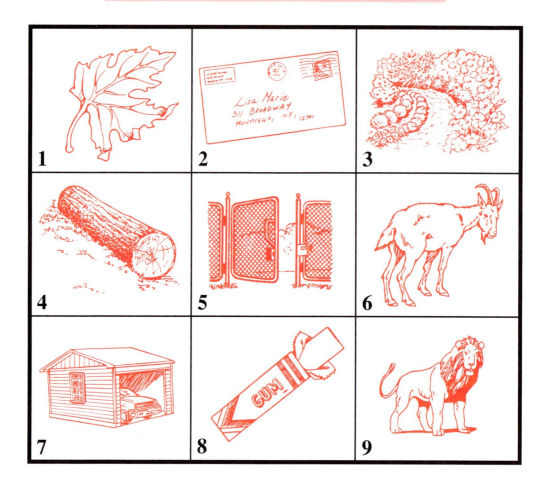

1. This **l**_____ fell off the tree.

2. Can you cut that **l**_____ in half?

3. "Yes, I like **g**_____," said Nick.

4. Give the **g**_____ something to eat.

5. Please close the **g**_____.

6. Will you write a **l**_____ to her?

1. I can write with a **p**_____ .

2. We heard the song on the **r**_____ .

3. Rosa put water in the **p**_____ .

4. Who took the **p**_____ off my bed?

5. Ann's pet **p**_____ can say good-by.

6. He has a **r**_____ on his finger.

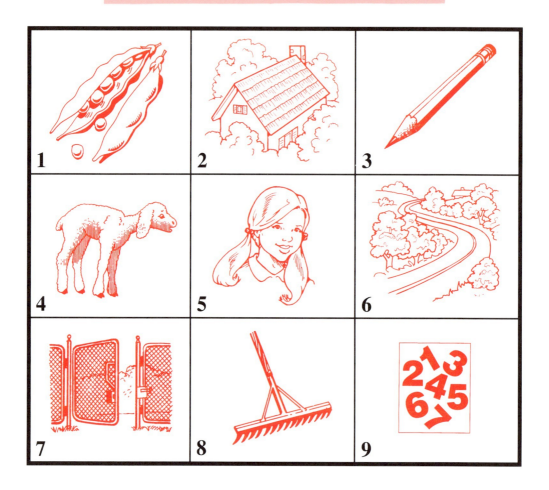

1. What color is the **r**_____ on your house?

2. I will need a **p**_____ to write.

3. Do you like to eat **p**_____?

4. The new **g**_____ came to Rosa's party.

5. The boys saw a **l**_____ on the farm.

6. We can walk down this **r**_____.

1. **N**_____ girls are in the house.

2. Mother reads the **n**_____ at night.

3. Is there water in the **k**_____?

4. Jerry got some **n**_____ to eat.

5. Molly and Sam have a pet **k**_____.

6. The **k**_____ will fly high in the sky.

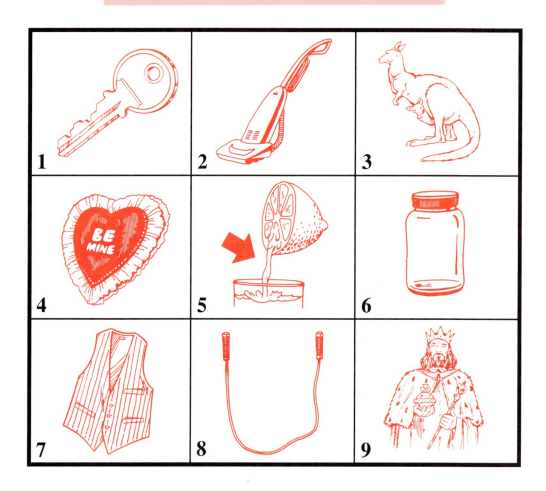

1. Put the candy in the **j**_____ .

2. She likes to jump with a **j**_____ .

3. I can jump like a **k**_____ .

4. What color **v**_____ are you wearing?

5. Tom sent Ann a **v**_____ .

6. Mother had the **k**_____ to the car.

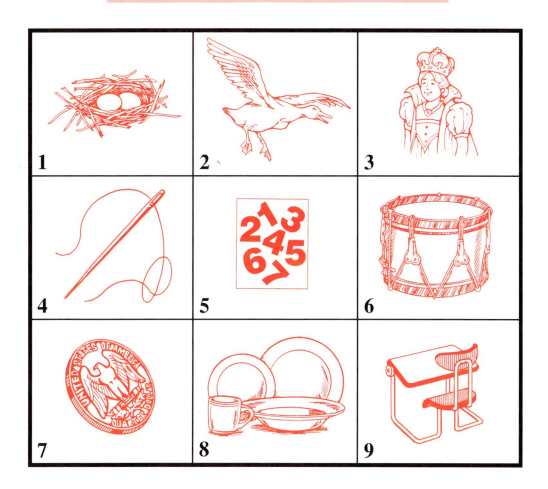

1. Please wash the **d**_____ after we eat.

2. There are **n**_____ in her book.

3. That woman is a **qu**_____ .

4. He paid a **qu**_____ for the toy.

5. I saw a **d**_____ on the farm.

6. We saw a **n**_____ in the tree.

1. I ate only one **d**_____.

2. She made a dress for her **d**_____.

3. The **z**_____ on his pants is broken.

4. Give the water to the big **d**_____.

5. We saw a tiger at the **z**_____.

6. Make the **y**_____ go up and down.

26

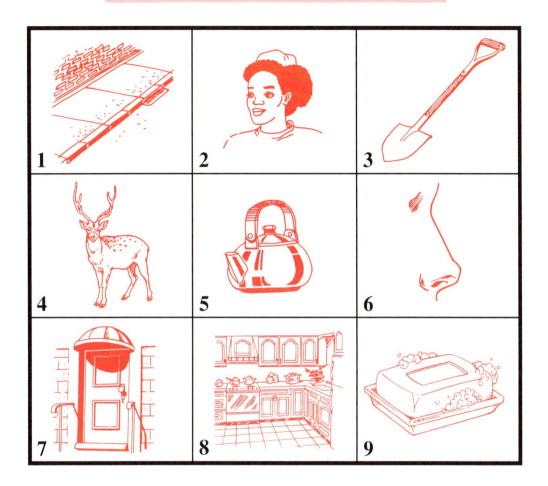

1. Please open the **d**_____ .

2. Bob and Ann are in the **k**_____ .

3. That **d**_____ can run very fast.

4. Wash your hands with the **s**_____ .

5. Who would like to be a **n**_____?

6. I rode my bike on the **s**_____ .

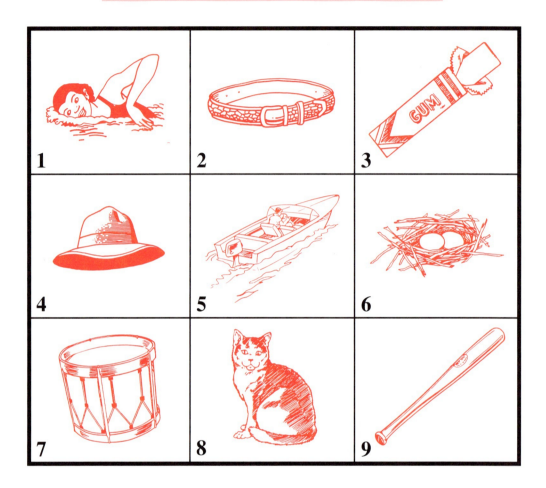

1. Father had a _____**t** on his head.

2. Mother got _____**m** for all of us.

3. We went for a ride in the _____**t**.

4. Do not bang on that _____**m**.

5. Steve saw a bird's _____**t** in the tree.

6. Ann knows how to _____**m**.

1. I caught a fish with this _____**k**.

2. I saw a _____**k** swim in the water.

3. Pat has a pretty new _____**s**.

4. Did you read this _____**k**?

5. I got her a _____**s** of water.

6. They will make a _____**k** house.

1. The _____**k** tells us the time.

2. What do they grow on that _____**m**?

3. He put on his new _____**t**.

4. Pam likes to bang on the _____**m**.

5. We went for a ride on a _____**s**.

6. We will sleep in the _____**t**.

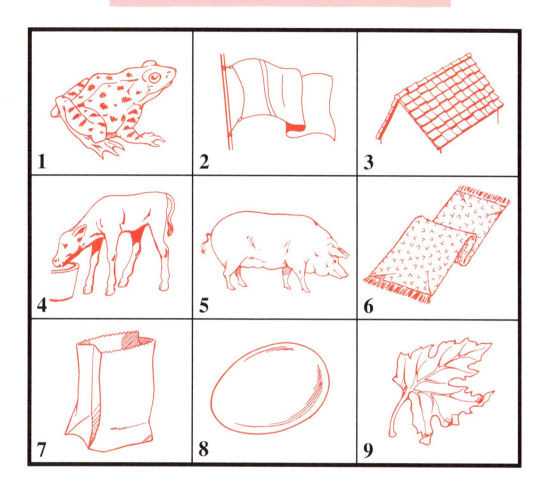

1. We saw a baby _____**f** at the farm.

2. You can cook an _____**g** many ways.

3. Not one _____**f** was on the tree.

4. I will carry the food in this _____**g**.

5. Our house needs a new _____**f**.

6. The _____**g** jumped into the water.

A. Exercising Your Skill

Name each picture below. Listen to the beginning and end sounds. What is the same? What is different?

Write the letter that stands for the beginning sound in the pictures. Write the letters that stand for the end sounds.

Write the letter that stands for the beginning sound in the pictures. Write the letters that stand for the end sounds.

B. Expanding Your Skill

Add a new beginning or end sound to the group of letters below. One is done for you. Use your paper.

$$\text{ca}\underline{n} \qquad \underline{\ }\text{up} \qquad \text{cu}\underline{\ } \qquad \underline{\ }\text{at}$$
$$\underline{\ }\text{all} \qquad \text{boo}\underline{\ } \qquad \text{ba}\underline{\ } \qquad \underline{\ }\text{in}$$

32

C. Exploring Language

Copy the chart below. Write a word in each box. Make your word name the thing listed on the left. Make it begin with the sound at the top. One is done for you.

	g	b	r
an animal	goat		
a color	green		
a person's name	Gary		

D. Expressing Yourself

Make picture riddles. Draw pictures of different things. Write the first letter or the last letter of the name of the picture. (The name will look like this: g____ or ____g.) See who can guess what your picture is.

1. Jenny went down the hill on a _____ **d**.

2. In _____**n** days we will go away.

3. Father put the food into the _____**n**.

4. Did you cut your _____**d**?

5. The funny _____**n** made us laugh.

6. Jack said, "I like to eat _____**n**."

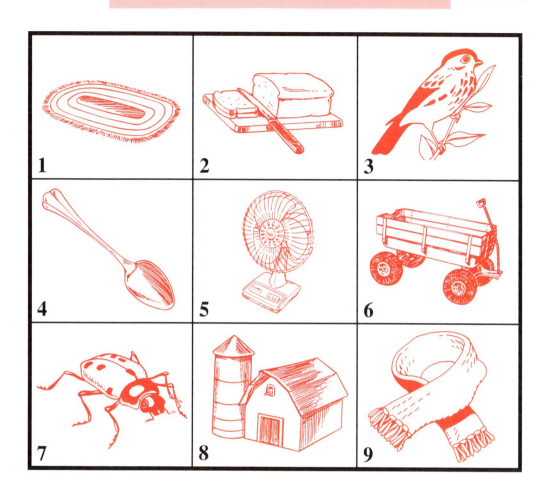

1. The cows are in the _____**n**.

2. Mother got a _____**g** for the floor.

3. Will you wear that _____**f**?

4. The baby can now eat with a _____**n**.

5. A little _____**d** was in the tree.

6. Juan went for a ride in the _____**n**.

1. You can see better by this _____p.

2. A _____l can run very fast.

3. Tom drank the milk in the _____p.

4. Can you kick the _____l?

5. The _____l came off the wagon.

6. The baby will play with the _____l.

1. We will put the candy into the _____r.

2. Did you read that _____k?

3. Put the toys in the _____x.

4. Can you open this _____k?

5. At night we can see a _____r.

6. My house has a back _____r.

1. Put a _____p on your letter.

2. Can you hear the _____l?

3. Mother sat down in the _____r.

4. Who does that _____l look like?

5. I put on my _____p and went out.

6. The _____k is on the wall.

1. Two _____ will walk home with me.

    (A) girl   **(B) girls**

2. Mary takes a _____ to school.

    (A) toy   **(B) toys**

3. One of the _____ is on the boat.

    (A) girl   **(B) girls**

4. Dad has a big _____ for me.

    (A) cake   **(B) cakes**

5. They are playing with a _____ .

    (A) ball   **(B) balls**

6. Rosa and I saw three _____ .

    (A) cat   **(B) cats**

1. He said, "I want to _____ that."

    (A) eat   (B) eats

2. Ron likes to _____ with him.

    (A) play   (B) plays

3. Sue _____ too fast for me.

    (A) walk   (B) walks

4. Tom will _____ you after school.

    (A) call   (B) calls

5. Jan _____ to go to school.

    (A) like   (B) likes

6. Will you _____ for my dog?

    (A) look   (B) looks

1. Here _____ Juan into the school.

      (A) come   **(B) comes**

2. Can you _____ that airplane?

      (A) see   **(B) sees**

3. Please _____ a box for me.

      (A) get   **(B) gets**

4. He will _____ us go with him.

      (A) let   **(B) lets**

5. I can't _____ my toys.

      (A) find   **(B) finds**

6. Betty _____ to play with him.

      (A) like   **(B) likes**

1. Father has a funny way of _____ .

    (A) laugh   **(B) laughing**

2. She said, "He can _____ too."

    (A) go   **(B) going**

3. Rosa said, "He is _____ too fast."

    (A) eat   **(B) eating**

4. Mother was _____ the girls.

    (A) call   **(B) calling**

5. Pat and I are _____ with the work.

    (A) help   **(B) helping**

6. The car is _____ at my house.

    (A) stop   **(B) stopping**

1. Jenny _____ to go to the farm.

       (A) want   **(B) wanted**

2. They have _____ with all of us.

       (A) play   **(B) played**

3. Sam and I helped Mother _____.

       (A) work   **(B) worked**

4. Can you _____ where Father is?

       (A) guess   **(B) guessed**

5. We all began to _____.

       (A) laugh   **(B) laughed**

6. The dog _____ on the bed.

       (A) jump   **(B) jumped**

1. We _____ where Juan is going.

   (A) know   **(B) knows**   **(C) knowing**

2. Mother is _____ for the boat.

   (A) look   **(B) looks**   **(C) looking**

3. Did they _____ working for you?

   (A) stop   **(B) stops**   **(C) stopping**

4. You can _____ it on the farm.

   (A) find   **(B) finds**   **(C) finding**

5. Did she _____ the little house?

   (A) see   **(B) sees**   **(C) seeing**

6. My dog is _____ in the house.

   (A) run   **(B) runs**   **(C) running**

1. She _____ at the boys and girls.

   (A) look   **(B) looked**   **(C) looking**

2. We will _____ to school with you.

   (A) walk   **(B) walks**   **(C) walking**

3. Pete _____ where Mother went.

   (A) guess   **(B) guessed**   **(C) guessing**

4. Rosa and her mother _____ fast.

   (A) work   **(B) works**   **(C) working**

5. She _____ her pet dog with her.

   (A) take   **(B) takes**   **(C) taking**

6. Ann is _____ a toy for me.

   (A) make   **(B) makes**   **(C) making**

1. Mother showed us how to _____ it.

    (A) lake   **(B) make**

2. You can _____ ducks on a farm.

    (A) find   **(B) kind**

3. Let's _____ Father to go with us.

    (A) get   **(B) pet**

4. It is time for us to go to _____ .

    (A) fed   **(B) bed**

5. When will the _____ come out?

    (A) run   **(B) sun**

6. We will sleep in the _____ .

    (A) tent   **(B) went**

1. What did the _____ eat?

       (A) goat   **(B) boat**

2. Kelly can run very _____.

       (A) past   **(B) fast**

3. "Come here _____," called Ben.

       (A) now   **(B) how**

4. Two _____ went into the house.

       (A) pen   **(B) men**

5. Dan _____ go to school with us.

       (A) pan   **(B) can**

6. I saw _____ walking to school.

       (A) Mike   **(B) like**

A. Exercising Your Skill

Look at the pictures below. Pick the word that names each picture correctly. Write the word on your paper.

soap or soaps?   towel or towels?

Now draw pictures to go with these words: **sinks**, **bathtub**, **ducks**.

B. Expanding Your Skill

Play "One baseball player, two baseball players." Pick a partner. Make up a sentence starting with "One ____ ." Your partner must say the same sentence, starting with "Two ____ ." ("One baseball player runs." "Two baseball players run.")

Take turns being the one who makes up the first sentence.

C. Exploring Language

Pick words from the boxes. Put them in the sentences to make a story. Add **-s**, **-ed**, or **-ing** if you need to. One is done for you.

Willy	float
Kids	clean
Soap	sail
A toy boat	play

Willy _cleans_ .

Willy _cleans_ today.

Willy _cleaned_ last week.

Willy loves _cleaning_ .

D. Expressing Yourself

Make a counting book. Draw pictures and write words. Go up to number 10.

Start with this: 1 boat floating
                    2 ducks swimming

1. Can you _____ what time it is?

    (A) well   **(B) tell**

2. They _____ to school in a car.

    (A) name   **(B) came**

3. Juan can _____ on the blue box.

    (A) jump   **(B) lump**

4. "Yes, you are _____ ," she said.

    (A) right   **(B) night**

5. Ann will _____ the boys.

    (A) tell   **(B) bell**

6. How did the spoon get _____?

    (A) bent   **(B) went**

1. She will _____ us have the books.

          (A) let   **(B) net**

2. Father will _____ us to school.

          (A) cake   **(B) take**

3. One _____ Pat came home with him.

          (A) pay   **(B) day**

4. I got him a _____ on airplanes.

          (A) book   **(B) cook**

5. Look out or you will _____.

          (A) wall   **(B) fall**

6. Will you _____ a cake for us?

          (A) rake   **(B) bake**

1. Do you see me _____ up here?

    (A) say   **(B) way**

---

2. A _____ is good to eat.

    (A) nut   **(B) hut**

---

3. Dan is in _____ of the house.

    (A) back   **(B) Jack**

---

4. Mother will get a blue _____.

    (A) far   **(B) car**

---

5. We will _____ down in the boat.

    (A) sit   **(B) it**

---

6. They are _____ going for a ride.

    (A) not   **(B) lot**

1. How did you break the _____?

    (A) toy   **(B) boy**

2. Tom was _____ on the way home.

    (A) sick   **(B) pick**

3. Bob and Pam like to play _____.

    (A) ball   **(B) hall**

4. Let's take a walk up the _____.

    (A) will   **(B) hill**

5. "Father got a _____," said John.

    (A) fat   **(B) hat**

6. Rosa did not _____ in the box.

    (A) took   **(B) look**

1. It's _____ to play in the sand.

   (A) run   **(B) fun**

---

2. Juan put his _____ into the jar.

   (A) and   **(B) hand**

---

3. She knows _____ to find the way.

   (A) how   **(B) cow**

---

4. Father _____ for a big book.

   (A) dent   **(B) sent**

---

5. _____ went to school with Ron.

   (A) Bill   **(B) Pill**

---

6. Ann went into her _____ .

   (A) house   **(B) mouse**

1. Put the _____ into the water.

      (A) net   **(B) get**

---

2. Tom sat in the _____ of the boat.

      (A) back   **(B) pack**

---

3. Pam was the _____ to come home.

      (A) past   **(B) last**

---

4. Mother put a picture on the _____ .

      (A) wall   **(B) tall**

---

5. We saw him _____ away in a car.

      (A) side   **(B) ride**

---

6. We will put the toys into a _____ .

      (A) sack   **(B) tack**

1. I will _____ for you at school.

     (A) hall   **(B) call**

2. Where can we _____ the red ball?

     (A) hide   **(B) wide**

3. Pam and Ron ran after the _____ .

     (A) fat   **(B) cat**

4. I know a _____ we can play.

     (A) same   **(B) game**

5. Your new coat is on the _____ .

     (A) hook   **(B) took**

6. I was too _____ to run and play.

     (A) got   **(B) hot**

1. Juan will _____ up the kitten.

   (A) pick   **(B) sick**

---

2. She said the dog was not in _____.

   (A) light   **(B) sight**

---

3. Ann can _____ the ball.

   (A) rat   **(B) bat**

---

4. We saw the horse eat the _____.

   (A) day   **(B) hay**

---

5. Bob put the baby into the play _____.

   (A) pen   **(B) ten**

---

6. They do not want to get _____.

   (A) let   **(B) wet**

1. It was time to go to **b**_____.

   (A) ed   **(B) ut**

2. Mother **c**_____ home from work.

   (A) at   **(B) ame**

3. It's **f**_____ to ride in a boat.

   (A) ind   **(B) un**

4. He got into the **b**_____ of the car.

   (A) oat   **(B) ack**

5. I can **m**_____ the boat go fast.

   (A) ake   **(B) an**

6. I can **t**_____ who he is.

   (A) ell   **(B) ake**

1. "Go **g**_____ Mother," said Tom.

         (A) et   **(B) ood**

2. We saw the **h**_____ at the farm.

         (A) ad   **(B) en**

3. We can not go out and play at **n**_____.

         (A) ight   **(B) ot**

4. "**L**_____ in back of you," he said.

         (A) et   **(B) ook**

5. That **b**_____ likes to play too.

         (A) all   **(B) oy**

6. I saw Meg **j**_____ into the water.

         (A) ump   **(B) ar**

1. Jenny will **r**_____ on her bike.

    (A) ide   **(B) ain**

2. Mother said we **w**_____ go there.

    (A) all   **(B) ill**

3. They are not very **f**_____ away.

    (A) ar   **(B) ell**

4. **T**_____ of us are here.

    (A) ook   **(B) en**

5. Father **t**_____ it with him.

    (A) ook   **(B) alk**

6. We will paint the **w**_____.

    (A) all   **(B) ent**

1. Rosa can find her **w**_____ home.

       (A) ay   **(B) ent**

2. She **c**_____ to play at my house.

       (A) ame   **(B) ake**

3. He said we will be with **R**_____.

       (A) id   **(B) ick**

4. Can you find the **b**_____ for me?

       (A) all   **(B) ig**

5. Where **c**_____ Juan and Ben be?

       (A) at   **(B) an**

6. Sam and Jill **w**_____ to the door.

       (A) ent   **(B) ay**

A. Exercising Your Skill

Name each picture below. Listen to the beginning sound.

Write the word that names the picture.

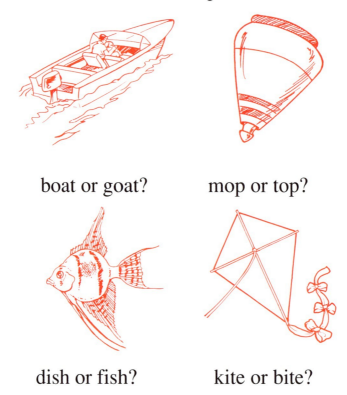

boat or goat?   mop or top?

dish or fish?   kite or bite?

B. Expanding Your Skill

Play a rhyming game. Say a word. The next player must say a word that rhymes. If you get stuck, try another word.

Start with **cat**...**bat**...

C. Exploring Language

Complete this poem. On your paper, write words that rhyme.

> Come play with me out in the sun.
> We both will have a lot of ____ .
> Jump the brook and then the wall.
> I will catch you if you ____ .
> We'll play some games and climb a tree
> And be good friends, just you and ____ .
> March and hop and sing a song.
> We'll play together all day ____ .

D. Expressing Yourself

Do one of these things.

1. Find a poem you like. Read it to the class.

2. Draw a rhyming picture. Some ideas are **fat cat in a hat** or **big pig dancing a jig**. Think up one of your own. Write a title for your picture.

CONCEPTS DEVELOPED